SHAWNA LUCKEY
Whispering Winds

Copyright @2020 by Shawna Luckey

All rights reserved. No part of this book may be reproduced in any form or by any electronic or mechanical means, including information storage and retrieval systems, without permission in writing from the publisher, except by reviewers, who may quote brief passages in a review.

This publication contains the opinions and ideas of its author. It is intended to provide helpful and informative material on the subjects addressed in the publication. The author and publisher specifically disclaim all responsibility for any liability, loss or risk, personal or otherwise, which is incurred as a consequence, directly or indirectly, of the use and application of any of the contents of this book.

WORKBOOK PRESS LLC
187 E Warm Springs Rd,
Suite B285, Las Vegas, NV 89119, USA

Website:	https://workbookpress.com/
Hotline:	1-888-818-4856
Email:	admin@workbookpress.com

Ordering Information:
Quantity sales. Special discounts are available on quantity purchases by corporations, associations, and others.
For details, contact the publisher at the address above.

ISBN-13:   978-1-953839-21-3 (Paperback Version)
            978-1-953839-22-0 (Digital Version)

REV. DATE: 22/09/2020

Contents

Dedication	7
Courage	9
Golden Glow	10
I Am With You	11
My One True Love	12
I am Free	13
	14
You are	15
Broken Heart	16
My Beautiful Niña	17
Beautiful Music	18
The Colors of Our Flag	19
Beautiful Rose Bud	20
My Cousin, My Sister	22
My Son	24
An Angels Heart	25
My Angel	26
Not Enough Time	27
Autumn Winter in Minutes	28
Our Tiniest Angel	29
My Golden Haired Beauty	30
Mother Nature	31
Our Little Angel in Pink	32
Our Earth Angel	33
Sister	34

....	.35
Gone Too Soon	.36
Nature..	.37
Sister Sun	.38
My Morning Glory	.39
My Heart Grows Heavy	.40
My Mother, My Angel	.41
I am .... I see	.42
Beautiful Hummingbird	.43
My Earth Angel..................................	.44
You are the Strongest	.45
Littlest Angel	.46
Brother Moon	.47
Missing You......................................	.48
My Hero	.49
Our Brother	.50
Our Angel with the Sunset Hair	.51
I Have an Angel Watching Over Me. ..	.52
Our Ebony Haired Beauty	.54
You are Me, I am You	.55
My Courageous Hero	.56
Bonded with Love	.57
Deadly ride, Forever17	.58
Peace	.59

Shawna Luckey

Dedication

I am dedicating this book to my Dad and Mom who taught me that daydreaming has meaning, to my 3 sisters and brother Kathy, Donnie, Mary and Jennifer, who have pushed me always to be the best when doing anything I set my mind too.

To my Husband and children who supported me through every adventure.

To my beautiful Sister in my heart, Rebecca who taught me to spread my wings and turn up the volume of my voice, to always listen to my heart.

To my Beautiful Granddaughter Marabella who teaches me every day to feel young.

Whispering Winds

Shawna Luckey

Courage

*I listen as you talk of all your hopes and dreams,
they never fall on deaf ears.
Pull the courage up from out of the darkest hiding place.
Relieve all our memories, shared memories are eternal.
Like the never-ending ripple of the skipping stone.
Remember the laughing, crying, loving shared memories.
This gives your heavy heart wings.
I love you forever more!*

Golden Glow

The fire in your heart has no more flame, flicker, no more glow.
The beauty of the flame is hidden.
Even when you remove the heavy mask you wear.
You are on your knees weeping, screaming, heartbroken, devastated, will the nightmare end?
I am kneeling beside you,
my arms holding a grip none other can break.
My glowing golden wings envelope us in the warm loving soft light.
The glow of the soft light will rekindle your heart to the fire it once was.
Always by your side to carry you when the burden is too great.
I am always loving you!!!

Shawna Luckey

I Am With You

My darling girl, from the time I returned to my heavenly home,
I have visited you every minute of every day.
Throughout it all, the long harsh times,
the happy, the sad times.
I have been by your side.
Holding you when the tears fall and your heart is heavy.
I am free and spread my angel wings, and soar like a bird.
I send you the sunshine to wrap you in a hug from me,
to warm you from head to toe.
When the wind blows I whisper I love you,
if you listen close, you will hear it.
I will never leave you.
When it is your time to return home,
I will be waiting with open arms.
I love you.

My One True Love

My beautiful Carmel colored Goddess.
Our heart strings are forever intertwined, never to be severed.
The fates have brought us together, to be forever intertwined.
Yet life has a cruel way of interfering in the fates plans,
life has separated us, on this earthly plain.
I won't bow down to the cruelty of life.
I will always be with you.
I am in the wind that blows your strawberry locks, I am in the sun that kisses your beautiful caramel cheek.
I am in the diamond drops of the rain.
Our love will always bloom, like the early spring flower as it opens to say hello.
We are together forever intertwined in our heart strings.
I am always here with you.
I love you……..

I am free

I am free from the sadness of this crazy world. I will sing the angels' choir.
Do not let your heart be heavy with grief.
I will wipe the tears that fall down your cheeks like a raindrop racing to get the bottom of a window.
I will soar through the sky like the mighty eagle.
I will wrap your heavy heart in my arms.
I will give you warmth like that of the California sun.
I will walk with you.
I will protect your heart from the burden of grief.
When the wind blows you will hear my whispers of I love you.
When the sun shines you always see my smile.
Always remember me with laughter.
Keep my memory alive.
Until we meet again.

You are....

You are my sunshine in the daytime.
You are the moonlight on a dark night.
You are the warmth when it's cold outside.
You are my rainbow on a rainy day.
You are the love that fills my heart, like the helium in a balloon.
You are the one who turns my frown, upside down.
When I have had a bad day, you are my happiness.
You are all that is right with the world.
You are……..my grandchild.

Shawna Luckey

Broken Heart

The pieces fall one by one crashing to the floor.
The tears fall like icicles.
Your knees give way to the weight of your broken heart.
A broken heart cannot mended.
A broken heart cannot love.
A broken heart cannot find peace.
A broken heart can be renewed.
A broken heart can be glued together with love and understanding, and compassion.
You can fix a broken heart with I love you.

My Beautiful Niña

Your heart is heavy with the burden of my passing.
I am not gone.
I walk with you every day, always by your side.
When you can't stand the pain no more, your heart feels like 100lb weight.
I wrap my angel wings around you to lighten your burden.
When the sun shines know that is me showing you how proud I am of you.
Do not cry for me daughter for I am free.
Free of the pain and agony.
I sing with the angel's choir.
I am here always; I know you feel my warm loving touch.
I kiss your cheek ever so lightly to dry your tears.
Your work here is not done.
'Till we stand face to face once again, I am waiting for you.
I love you so much.
I am so proud of you.
All my love, Mom.

Beautiful Music

My beautiful music comes not from a man-made instrument.
My beautiful music comes from the wind
as it blows through the trees.
My beautiful music comes from the birds as they sing.
My beautiful music comes from the wind chimes when they
dance in the wind as it blows.
My beautiful music comes from my heart as it is full of love,
with the music all around me.
My beautiful music comes from the birds as they soar through
the clouds.
There is beauty in everything if you just sit, in the grass, just
listening, amongst the trees.
God gives us all his music if you just stop and listen with your
heart.
My beautiful music is sitting and listening to your earth angel
tells you a story about their life.
Thank you God for the music of the world.
Don't ever stop listening to the beautiful music.

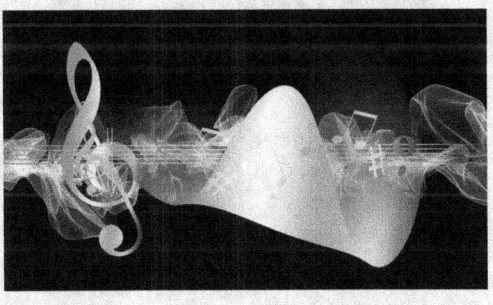

The Colors of Our Flag

The red, white, and blue are not just colors.
They have such a true meaning for people in America.
They stand for freedom, they stand for sacrifice.
God blesses these three colors each and every day.
Red is the blood shed during each and every war.
White is the color of the angel wings the soldiers sprout after losing the battle.
Blue is the tears of the loved ones missing those soldiers that became angels.
These three colors alone stand for so much.
Together they stand for the freedom of each and every American.
God bless our soldiers fighting to keep those colors important and with the true meaning.

Shawna Luckey

Beautiful Rose Bud

Look at this tiny rose bud.
Through the years the angels have helped it to bloom into the
most beautiful unique rose you have ever seen.
The rainbow is in awe of all the shade of the petals.
You are the rose; you have bloomed into the most beautiful
young lady, spread your wings and soar.
Follow the whispers of your heart.
The angels will guide you.
Only you can determine how the rose blooms.
The world is open to your hopes and dreams…
Much love……

My Cousin, My Sister

You were a ray of sunshine my beautiful bronze angel, you had sunlight in your smile.
My heart skipped a beat every time I saw you, we are so close you are my sister in God.
We are bound in blood.
I know when you are here, the sun shines, and my heart is as light as the feather from your angel wings.
My heart is so heavy from missing you.
Let your golden wings spread as wide as the ocean, take flight and soar freely.
You are free from the heart ache from this sad world.
I know you walk with me every day. I can feel your hugs when the sun shines.
It warms my heart, even on the coldest days.
The wind whispers I love you" to me.
Soar through the fluffy cotton clouds.
Be free until we meet again.

Shawna Luckey

My Son....

The first mention of you, I was so elated to hear I would be having you my first born.
I placed a soft kiss on your forehead to say hi, I am your mommy.
I am so proud of you my heart overflows with love like a fountain on a hot summer day.
You walk with a halo of sunshine everywhere you go.
You have such an angelic personality .
Everywhere you venture people are drawn to you like a magnet.
The mere mention of your name leaves me breathless.
When you love, you love with every essence of your being.
Don't ever lose the sparkle in your eye.
I love you…Mom.

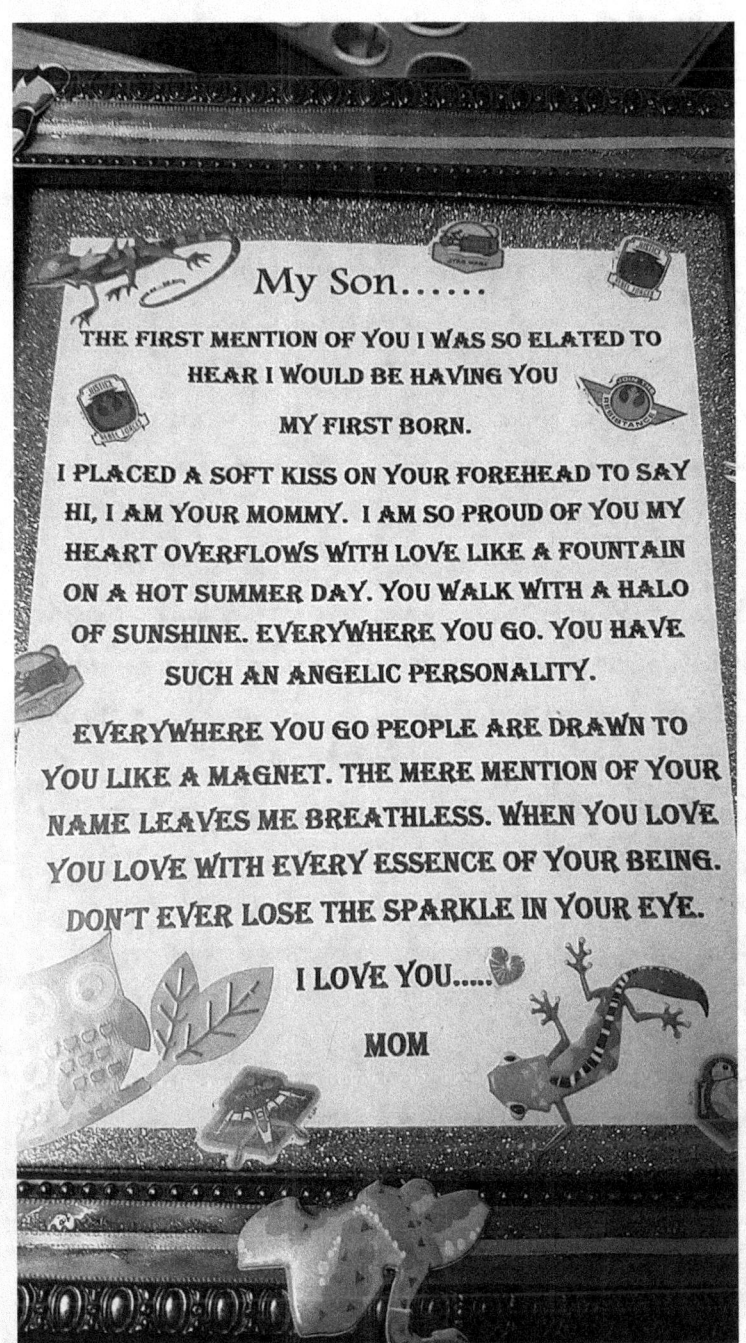

An Angels Heart

My saving grace has a beautiful soul.
When she talks the trees and flowers dance to the music of her voice.
The fairies come to hear her speak.
The wind and the clouds come to hear what she is saying.
When she smiles the sun smiles, the sun's rays are brighter.
She always stays to help another soul be free.
When she thanks a soldier the world is a better place.
She has followers wherever she goes, they soak up her aura.
Yet when she cries, the flowers and the trees weep with her.
The wind blows to dry her tears. She puts everyone before herself.
When she is around me in my world the heavy burden is lifted.
The fairies know her by name.
They hug her every day.

Shawna Luckey

My Angel

I have an angel watching over me.
Her wings spread as she flies high in the sky like the birds that are free to soar through the clouds.
My angel I see a neon green sparkle in your wings, like glitter in the sun.
I see pink diamond sparkles in your hair.
Your gown flows with turquoise like that of an evening sky just before a storm.
You see the tear glisten on my cheeks.
I feel that ever so soft kiss you leave on my tear filled cheeks.
yes my angel I hear you whisper in the wind ...
Mom I love you.

Not Enough Time

Even if you lived to be a 100 years old that would be too soon for you to go.
My heart breaks into a million pieces every time I think of you.
Like a glass, shattering to the floor.
A puzzle I will never be able to put together.
There will always be that one missing piece.
I know in my heart you are free, free from the pain, free to soar through the clouds like a hawk.
When the sun shines I catch a glimpse of your golden wings.
I hear your whispers in the wind, the wind blows I hear "I love you, I am always with you, and I walk beside you very day".
At night when I am alone, the tears fall like a waterfall.
I feel your soft touch as you wipe away the tears from my cheek.
I feel your soft hug when times get so unbearable.

Shawna Luckey

Autumn Winter in Minutes

There are so many colors of autumn,
the reds, golds, greens and oranges.
The wonder of the colors is amazing,
just when you think there is nothing more beautiful.
God amazes you with the purest color of all, white.
Before your very eyes he can change your world
with a blanket of snow in a matter of minutes.
You start a whole new day and it changes just like that.

Our Tiniest Angel

Our tiniest angel.
Mommy and Daddy love you so much.
You have not been with us long,
before you gained your angel wings.
We will open the door to our hearts where you will be tucked
away, always remembered, never forgotten.
You will be with us always, until we meet again.

Shawna Luckey

My Golden Haired Beauty

You were everybody's sunshine on a rainy day.
No one was a stranger to you.
Our time was too short.
You were so young when God called you home.
I find myself in a field of yellow daisies.
I close my eyes, I hear the wind whisper.
I love you, in my ear as a tear rolls down my check I feel your soft caress, wipe away my tears, they fall like a waterfall.
I open my eyes to see your beautiful wings extended far and wide.
In your extended wings I see the sunshine specks of gold that sparkle in the sun.
Your halo is pink with gold and blue glitter shimmering in the sunlight.
You tell me you will always be with me.
You love me always and forever.
As you start to take flight your beautiful wings block out the sun so I can see your angelic wink you blow me a kiss, and your smile warms my heart.
I will always love you My Golden Haired Beauty.

Mother Nature

You love us so much; you give us such wondrous colors and such wondrous beings.
Such light that is so beautiful it makes everybody happy.
You give us such love when we are hot; you blow a soft wind to cool us.
When we are cold you give us extra warm seasons to remind us of what we love.
You paint us with those wonderful colors.
You give us shade with the clouds.
You have an enormous wrath when you are angry we can see it in your tornados and floods.
You keep all your creations fulfilled with water and nourishments.
You are our mother nature. We must take care of you.

Shawna Luckey

Our Little Angel in Pink

**You are free to skip among the flowers, dance with the butterflies, fly with the wind, sing with the birds.
You are as light as feather from your angel wings. Your halo sparkles in the sunlight, like gold and silver glitter.
You can slide down a rainbow with the angels.
You are free to soar through the clouds.
Be free our little Angel in Pink.**

Our Earth Angel

Our hearts are breaking into a million pieces.
You fought the good fight.
You fought with bravery and such courage and you fought with such grace.
You will be able to sing Amazing Grace with the Angels.
You can spread your iridescent Angel wings and soar.
You will be with us always.
You were a part our hearts and always will be.
We will miss you, we love you so.
You are in pain no more.
You will dry our tears as they fall.
You are with Mother and Father again. You were our Earth Angel, you are now Heavens Angel until we meet again.........

Sister

You are not my sister by blood, yet we are still sisters.
You and I are sisters by souls.
Your skin is bronzed by the sun.
My skin is white as the snow.
Your hair is long black as the midnight sky.
My hair is golden as the sunshine.
Your legs, your arms, your body is long and slender and beautiful.
My legs, my arms, my body is short and stumpy and cute.
We were not born of the same mother in this life yet we still found each other.
Again we are sisters by choice….my sister.

Infuse your sorrows with the tree,
no more will they be.
The tree will blossom new life
as your sorrows will no longer be.
Float, weightless on the waves of the ocean,
let them carry your broken heart to sea.
To be reborn and inflate your heart
with the love you have from me will be.
Kiss the sunflower.
Let the glow from the warmth
wash away the cloud of sadness you hold for me.
Your heart is reborn like the blossoms of the tree.

Shawna Luckey

The white crested waves roll like a log.
They are so white against the blue sky,
the sky is as blue as the deep sea.
I imagine myself riding those waves.
I fell so free, free as a bird when it's flying,
arms spread wide like wings
that catch the beautiful breeze of the wind.
With the hushed whispers of the wind,
I hear the Angels songs, as they fly high.
Ever soaring, the angel wings glistening in the sun.

Gone Too Soon

What could have gone wrong? You left us too soon.
Why couldn't we see through the fog of your emotions?
They took you from us: you were silently crying out for help,
we never heard your pain.
Now you are free of this pain and anguish.
Spread your rainbow angel wings.
Fly like a dove, free as the wind in the trees.
Be free to soar through the clouds.
When the sun shines we will see your smile.
It will always dry our tears and warm our hearts until we see
each other again…

Shawna Luckey

Nature

The sound of the rain is like little angel feet.
Pitter-patter on the roof.
The lightning is the angels playing
with the light switch in the sky.
The thunder is like God running to tickle
the little angels for playing with the light switch.
The wind is like the angels whispering a secret in your ear.
The sun is like the smile from an angel.

Whispering Winds

Sister Sun

Sister sun warms you with her hugs.
Sister sun brightens your day.
Sister sun smiles like a sister
after being distant for such a long time.
The sun always smiles like a sister
who has seen you for the first after a long absence.

Shawna Luckey

My Morning Glory

You were my Morning Glory, although you are gone.
I seem to carry you in my heart every minute of every day. I can imagine your Angel wings Glistening in the sun. My tears Fall like a waterfall, I sit and look at your picture, I can't even grasp where the time went.
From the first time I held you in my arms to the last hug I ever gave you.
It seems like a light year.
Now it feels like an eternity 'till we meet again.
My heart is breaking into million pieces.
I can't find the glue to put it back together.
Your smile lit up a room, always glowing with happiness.
I see you in my dreams standing in a field of wildflowers calling to me, Mom, come on lets go have a picnic.
Now all that is left is sadness and Heart break.
If I could catch a ride on a cloud or a rainbow just to get to you I would, just to be with you for eternity.
You are free to spread your wings and fly.

My Heart Grows Heavy...

As I walk this broken road of life, with a painted smile, my heart grows heavy.
My eyes overflow with oceans of tears that roll down my blistered cheeks, like an acid waterfall.
I cry for the tiny angels being tortured and twisted by their very protectors.
I cry for the young people who run away from their broken home — to unwillingly sell their bodies for food and shelter.
I cry for our soldiers fighting bravely for world peace — to only return home shattered and broken by the blackness of war.
I cry for all the helpless animals being maimed and beaten, when they only hold love in their hearts.
I cry for Mother Earth.
She is so beaten and broken. I cry for you,
you who do not know me.
My heart grows heavy...

Shawna Luckey

My Mother, My Angel

*You are my angel, you hold me in your soft wings.
When I cried you wipe my tears with your angelic gown.
You soar through the air with no pain.
You can now sing with the choir of angels.
You can teach all the little angels.
When you were on the earth, you were our earth angel.
You lifted us up when we were sad.
You always had warm hugs and a smile as bright as the sunshine.
You made our home always so warm and inviting.
Thank you My Mother, My Angel.
I love you, My Angel.*

I am ... I see...

I look at my reflection, you are there staring back at me.
I look at my hands, they are your hands.
I look at my feet, they are your feet.
I see my hair blowing in the wind, it is your hair.
When I laugh, it is your laugh.
When I hug, it is your arms hugging.
When I sing, it is your voice.
When I look at me, it is you.
When I see my reflection, it is your reflection.
I am you….Mom.
I am you….Dad.

Shawna Luckey

Beautiful Hummingbird

*The tears fall from our eyes like rain from the clouds.
You are free, free from the heavy burden that has consumed
your heart for far too long.
We will look over the rainbow each time and listen in the wind
as it blows to hear your whispers of "I love you.
We will know it is you hugging us when the sun shines.
We will feel you always around us on those hard days when we
just don't think we can make it through, you are our strength.
Be free to soar through the clouds like that of the mighty eagle.
Fly free like the butterfly; flitter ever so softly like the
hummingbird.
Until we arrive at the reunion keep us all safe here on earth.
I love you sweet angel.*

Whispering Winds

My Earth Angel

*Earth Angels are a sign from God,
that there is still goodness in the world.
You are my brave Earth Angel.
Your smile lights up the world like the sunshine lights the
gloomy day after a cold rain,
you have Angel Wings the color of a rainbow
they shimmer in Sunlight.
When I see you my Friend My Heart warms with such Joy at
what a beautiful soul you have.
You are going through such a hard thing right now.
Yet you always have a smile on your face.* **God will hold you in
his arms when the burden is so heavy.
God Bless you My friend.**

Shawna Luckey

You are the Strongest

You stand tall. You are green, yellow, white, red, orange.
You are standing to attention like a soldier.
You never fall; you stand firmly on the ground.
When you are young you can be pushed around.
When you are older you grow more and more sturdy.
You can be bent in different shapes.
You are in different shapes.
You are all different sizes.
Nature binds you to her will; you just go with the flow always leaning to the push of the wind.
It is a tug of war between you and the wind. You almost always win.
Sometimes at sad times the wind wins.
You are forever broken and twisted in unnatural shapes and positions.
You bend at the will of the wind.
Almost always never breaking, until big brother comes a calling, then that bully rushes you right over until you are a broken heap.
Fire and lightning are your enemies.

Littlest Angel

*We are your mommy and daddy.
We love you even if we can't hold you,
your wings will spread no matter what.
You will return to heaven in Gods arms,
you will watch over us all safe.
Big sissy loves you too,
wait for mommy and daddy we will all be together again someday.
Littlest Angel kisses and hugs in the wind.*

Shawna Luckey

Brother Moon

The moon wraps you in his strong arms at night.
He stands tall to protect you.
He can be there a quarter of the time.
He can hide and just remain in the shadows as a silent protector

Missing You

You left me alone.
You left me to fend for myself.
Why did you have to go so soon?
I am missing you like I miss the sun on a rainy day.
I am missing you like I miss a long, lost friend.
I am missing you like you miss your breath when you are under water.
I called you, why won't you answer?
Where are you?
I start to cry.
My tears fall like a waterfall.
My heart is squeezing so bad.
I can't stand it.
Why are you gone?
Where are you?
I can't hear you anymore.
Where did you go?
Why did you leave me?
I will wait by my phone, I can't exist anymore.
Where are you?
I don't know.
Please contact me and tell me where you are.
Why can't I find you?
Why are you gone?
Oh my heart is crushing.
Why are you gone?
Where are you?
I am missing you.
You had to go home to your real home.

I am missing you.

Shawna Luckey

My Hero

*Though you are gone, I am being as strong as I can be for mom.
You are my hero: you are my sunshine on a rainy day.
I see you smile when the sun shines each day.
We were together always.
Now you are here only in my heart.
I see the beautiful signs you leave me to say " I am always here".
"I love you" I see you in my dreams, I see you in a strangers smile yet I cannot hug you when I hug mom it's like hugging you both at the same time.
Now you are an angel, you show me when I catch a glimpse of a white butterfly.
When I see the rainbow so vibrant, I see you sending your love.
I'm missing you each every day.
I ask you to please show me another sign.
I am crying, I feel your soft touch wipe the tears.
I hear a song that reminds me of you, it also makes you forever dad.
'Till we are together again in heavens home.*

Our Brother

You are strong; you are protector in the absence of our father.
Your laugh is yours,
yet it echoes with the sound of dad.
You will fight anyone who speaks ill of your sisters.
Your laugh is yours, yet it echoes with the sound of da
Your features, your hands mirrors our dads.
When I look at you my heart floats
from the heavy burden of grief.
You are our brother.
When you smile I see the sunshine in your eyes
telling me you are happy.
Your voice carries through the wind,
just as if it was our dad's voice.
You are a father now your son's voice will carry through the wind-like his fathers' and grandfathers before him…. We love you Brother.

Shawna Luckey

Our Angel with the Sunset Hair

You have no more sadness.
We know you watch over us every day.
We see your smile in the sun.
We feel your breath when the wind blows.
You dry our tears as they flow like a leaking faucet down our cheeks.
You know when our hearts are breaking into a million pieces because we have seen the beautiful miracles you send us every day.
As the moon light blankets us we feel your warm arms holding us as we dream.
We feel your kiss upon our foreheads as we fall into a restful sleep.
We love our Sunset haired Angel.

Whispering Winds

I Have an Angel Watching Over Me

Her wings spread as she flies high in the sky like the birds that are free to soar through the clouds.
My Angel, I see a neon Green Sparkle in your wings like glitter in the sun.
I see pink diamond sparkles in your hair.
Your gown flows with turquoise like that of an evening sky in a storm.
You see the glisten on my cheeks.
I feel that ever so soft.
Kiss you leave on my tear filled cheek.
Yes my Angel girl.
I hear you whisper in the wind.
I love you.
Our Earth Angel
Your wings were hidden by your uniform, they spread as soon as the call of your name is heard you instantly became what God intended you to be.
An Earth Angel to so many lives.
Fire fighters and EMTs are here as Earth Angels.
Why then did he take you so soon.
I am living without you.
Every breath I take that you cannot is hard.

Shawna Luckey

When it gets to be so unbearable I feel a warm peaceful feeling coming over me, I know it is you wrapping me in your wings lifting my heavy heart.
Your Angel wings are my protection form heartache.
You soar through the clouds like an Eagle on the hunt. Be free to soar.
Only to visit me in my dreams.
Ride a rainbow, sing with the Angels.
Forever my Earth Angel.

Our Ebony Haired Beauty

Your Hair is as dark as the stormy sky.
You are as beautiful as the sun when it plays peek a boo through the clouds after a storm has lifted.
I smell your perfume and turn to see if you are here yet you are Not.
A tear forms on my cheek like a rain drop on a window.
I feel a soft feathery touch on my arm, I know it is you giving me comfort from this heavy burden.
Your silver wings glistening in the sun light as you soar through the clouds.
You walk with me every day to lift this 100 pound weight off my shoulders.
The wind blows and carries Angel whispers to tell me you are ok.
I can feel your soft touch on my head as I bow with such Heartache and grief.
Be free my Ebony HAIRED Angel, 'til we meet again.

Shawna Luckey

You are Me, I am You

You look at your reflection, I am there staring back at you.
You look at your hands, they are my hands.
You look at your feet, they are my feet.
You see your hair blowing in the wind, it is my hair.
When you laugh, it is my laugh.
When you hug, it is my arms hugging you
when you sing, I am singing.
When you look at you, it is me you see.
When I see my reflection, it is you I see.
You are me, I am you.
I love you Areeana, always and forever.
--Mom {2020} This one is for my daughter

My Courageous Hero

The moment you make the decision to fight for our freedom, is the most enormous sacrifice that one person can make.
You are mother, daughter, sister, brother, son, father, grandfather and grandmother, no matter who you are, you are an earth angel.
How does anyone say 'thank you'?
How do we show our gratitude to an earth angel like you, a hero like you?
Living your life guarded every minute of every day.
You have given so selflessly.
You are a hero to so many people.
Not enough people say thank you.
Be at peace earth angel with every step you take.

Shawna Luckey

Bonded with Love

*Your heart and soul are shattered
In to a million pieces
Remember me with sugar cookie kisses...
Remember me with huge Teddy Bear Hugs...
Remember my golden sunny smiles
Remember the sparkle you put in my eyes every time you were near.
Each memory you have of me mommy is the glue that bonds all the pieces back together again.
I walk by your side, I put my tiny hand in yours, each night I kiss your cheek...*

Deadly ride, forever 17

You took a deadly ride, September 23, 2012
Never knowing it would be your last hoorah, Forever 17
your wings always hidden,
are now spread wide as the heart can see.
I hear your smile everyday, The sunshines brighter. The clouds
part further at the mention of you.
I see the flitter of the hummingbird, my heart leaps.
I am always feeling your strength,
light as a feather on my heavy heart.
you are as close to my own as you ever will be.
Forever 17, Always a light behind your Beautiful Blue eyes.
Forever 17, Never to grow and take life by the reins.
Forever 17, Always my Earth angel. For eight years and
counting, always in my heart.

Shawna Luckey

Peace

*I sit in the quiet of the night hearing the song of the crickets.
Watching the clouds brush a sugary kiss over the moon.
I feel the heavy weights of the hussle and bussle from the day,
float away on a wave, from my crooked old tired body.
I feel like a youngster, running through the bountiful colors the
wildflowers illuminate with, Dreaming of the wonders the night
holds.
Not a dream, only a lively dance of the peaceful summer night
air.
this is the hearts hush. The souls rebirthing, to face another day,
full of hopes and dreams of all the waking souls in the glow of
the morning.*

www.ingramcontent.com/pod-product-compliance
Lightning Source LLC
Chambersburg PA
CBHW071409070526
44578CB00002B/531